Value in the Village

A Savings and Investment Club Guide for African-Americans

Celeste M. Moy, Esq.

Edited by
Moy-Savings Publications Committee

GATEWAY PRESS, INC.
Baltimore, MD 1998

Please direct all correspondence and book orders to:
MOY SAVINGS
PO Box 1112
Vienna, VA 22183-1112

Library of Congress Catalog Card Number 97-78332
ISBN 0-9663016-0-9

Published for the author by
Gateway Press, Inc.
1001 N. Calvert Street
Baltimore, MD 21202

Printed in the United States of America

Dedication

I dedicate this book to my husband Ed Street and my son Eddie Street, II without whose love, patience, indulgence and support this book never would have been completed; and to all the members of Moy-Savings and Investment Group, Inc. for their commitment and dedication to our organization; and most of all to my mom and dad, Melvin B. and Hazel V. Moy, without whose unwavering faith, vision, love and encouragement Moy-Savings would not exist.

TABLE OF CONTENTS

SAMPLE FORMS

address unfair lending practices, and no doubt the CRA will have to be amended again before we will see any measurable improvement in lending practices for African-Americans. Unfortunately, it is doubtful that a Republican-controlled Congress will pass stronger legislation to address discriminatory lending practices or strengthen the CRA, particularly in light of the banking industry's tremendous lobbying power.

The good news is, collectively African-Americans already have the economic power to do whatever we want or need to do for ourselves. We simply need to do a better job of pooling our economic power to accomplish our common goals and objectives. Our economic woes stem not from how much or how little money we make, but, rather, from how much we spend, where we spend it, and how little we save. Consider, for example, the results of a 1994 study by the University of Georgia which reports that African-Americans spent $399 billion dollars in 1994, which is almost the same as our total earnings for that year. In fact, the net worth of African-Americans (the ratio of household assets to liabilities) is nearly 10 times less than the net worth for all other Americans. While there are many factors contributing to the economic disparity between African-Americans and other Americans, chief among them is that too much of our income is spent on non-appreciating or depreciating assets, and not too little income. Too much of the income that enters the African-American community ends up leaving the community too soon. It has been estimated, for example, that a dollar changes hands 7 times in white communities as compared to 1.5 times in African-American communities.

The members of Moy-Savings and Investment Group, Inc. decided to seize greater control of their financial destiny and security by working together to increase the net worth of each of its members. We discovered that we can save a lot more, increase our individual net worth a lot faster, and achieve other common goals and objectives by pooling our resources and our talents. Every African-American family, church, sorority, fraternity, charitable organization, or social group can and should do the same by following a few easy steps. The following pages describe those steps as taken by the members of Moy-Savings and Investment Group, Inc.

CHAPTER
2

HOW TO START A SAVINGS CLUB

You will need 10 to 20 people to organize a savings club. First, it is critically important that your prospective members be committed to embarking upon a long-term investment program. If some members are committed to long-term investing while others are only interested in playing the market with quick buys and sells, the club is not going to last very long. According to the National Association of Investment Clubs ("NAIC") 40% of all investment clubs formed breakup within two years, usually because some members expect, wrongly, that an investment club is nothing more than a scheme to "get rich quick."[1] People who are willing to commit to a long term program of investment and financial study are the best prospects for membership. Secondly, try to identify people who will enjoy each other's company, as you are likely to have regular monthly, quarterly, and/or annual membership meetings. Some clubs

1 The NAIC is a Michigan, non-profit stock corporation located in Royal Oak, Michigan, operating to provide services to its members. For more information write to NAIC, P.O. Box 220, Royal Oak, MI 48068.

restrict membership to men or to women, while others admit both. According to the NAIC "all female" clubs have generally outperformed "all male" clubs, with a lifetime earning rate of 10.5% as compared to 9.7% for the men. Moy-Savings has benefitted tremendously from a diversity of occupations, experiences and talents among its male and female members. On the other hand, there are many successful clubs where all of the members belong to a single profession. Thirdly, the members must commit to a common investment philosophy which should be in writing and reviewed regularly in order to avoid fundamental disagreements about it later. Lastly, the Club should establish annual and long-term goals and objectives, and each member should be committed to achieving those goals and objectives.

Investment clubs may be set up either as partnerships or corporations. The partnership form appears to offer club members more tax advantages and is the form most commonly used. If most or all of your members are concerned about additional annual income tax liability, however, the corporate structure may be more appropriate. The corporate structure also provides you with a stock or membership certificate as tangible evidence of your membership. It is also possible to be organized as a corporation but treated as a partnership for tax purposes. If organized and treated as a corporation for tax purposes, an investment club's earnings could be taxed twice; once at the corporate level as income tax on the corporate earnings, and later the members may have to pay income tax on the allocation of corporate profit and earnings. Fortunately, you may be able to delay the second tax if the profit and earnings are reinvested rather than distributed to the members. (The benefits of reinvesting dividends are also discussed in Chapter 12). Partnerships, on the other hand, do not pay taxes. Instead, each partner is required to report his or her share of the Partnership's income for tax purposes every year.

Each club should consult an attorney and/or accountant to determine which structure is best, considering the financial status of the majority of its members.

Moy-Savings was formed on October 6, 1990 as a general partnership under the laws of the State of Michigan. (See Partnership Agreement at Form 1). Moy-Savings was originally conceived by its oldest member, Melvin B. Moy, and in many respects is a re-creation of a similar organization established by Mr. Moy with his father, uncles and brothers in the late 1940's. Partially as a result of the successful investment decisions of the Moy-Savings Investment Committee on behalf of the general membership, Moy-Savings was incorporated on February 1, 1994 as Moy-Savings and Investment Group, Inc., a Virginia corporation (See Form 5 for Articles of Incorporation).

Every club should have an operating agreement that sets forth the purpose of the Club, its goals and objectives, amount of minimum contributions, accounting procedures, membership rules and rights, withdrawals from membership, and any other desired rules of operation. (See Moy-Savings Partnership Agreement at Form 1).

You should choose a name that clearly identifies the purpose of the Club. And, you will need to elect at least four officers for purposes of conducting club meetings, conducting club affairs, and keeping the Club focused on its goals and objectives. The Club President may set the time and place for meetings, preside over meetings, set meeting agendas, and establish committees as needed or this may be done on a consensus basis at Club meetings. (See Form 2 for sample meeting agenda). You will need to elect a Vice-President to assume the President's duties in his or her absence. Some Clubs also require the Vice President to be responsible for providing or organizing investment educational presentations (no more than 15–20 minutes) at Club meetings. The minutes for each meeting should be prepared and presented by the Club's Secretary. (See Form 3 for sample Minutes). Of course, the minutes of the last meeting should be read at the beginning of each new meeting or sent to the membership in advance and approved at the following meeting. The members should be asked for corrections or additions, if any, and if there are none, the minutes should be approved as read or presented. In the interest of time, Moy-Savings sends copies of the minutes to each member prior to its meetings. At the meeting, the Secretary asks whether everyone received a copy of the minutes, and then, if so, whether there are any additions or corrections. When the members are given an opportunity to read the minutes beforehand, it's not necessary to spend time reading them again at the meeting. The Secretary is also responsible for keeping all of the Club's minutes and other types of correspondence, while the President is most likely to keep other official Club papers, such as the Club Agreement or Corporate Book. Finally, the Club will need a Financial Officer, who in many ways is the hardest working member of the Club. The Financial Officer is responsible for maintaining the Club's financial records, preparing periodic statements of the Club's receipts and disbursements, and most importantly, a record of each member's interest in the Club. (See Form 4 for sample Accounting Report). The Financial Officer is also responsible for preparing or having prepared, the annual tax information for each partner in a partnership, or the tax return for a corporation. The NAIC offers a great computer program to its members for club record keeping.

Moy-Savings has established the following goals and objectives for the Club: (1) to encourage thrift among its members; (2) to create a source of credit at fair and reasonable rates of interest; (3) to provide an opportunity to its members to use and control their own money in order to improve their economic and social condition; (4) to invest the assets of the Corporation in stocks, bonds, other securities, real estate and personalty; (5) to engage in any other activity and to provide any other service for the education and benefit of its members.

CHAPTER 3

How to Operate a Savings Club

Moy-Savings is a unique and exciting investment club that is truly unlike any other. We receive lots of requests to share our rules of operation with other clubs or would-be clubs, which we are happy to oblige. Investment clubs have existed in the United States for more than 80 years. The oldest known club began in Texas in 1898. The earlier clubs were primarily elite social groups blessed with large sums of money to engage in investment and speculation. It was not until 1940 that circumstances spurred development of the modern investment club. The late Frederick C. Russell, unable to find a job and desiring to buy a small business, decided to form an investment club as the vehicle for accumulating the capital he needed. As a result, the Mutual Investment Club of Detroit was formed, and it determined to do four things:

1. invest every month;
2. reinvest all dividends;
3. buy stock in growth companies;
4. diversify its investments.

Ironically, around the same time Moy-Savings' Melvin B. Moy was forming his first family investment group in Detroit. A few years later on October 20, 1951 the National Association of Investment Clubs ("NAIC") also was founded in Detroit, Michigan. NAIC is a not-for-profit organization that assists individual investors and clubs in organizing, investing, and managing their portfolios. Moy-Savings is a member of NAIC, and highly recommends membership to any investment club interest group.

Like traditional investment clubs, the members of Moy-Savings make monthly contributions which are deposited into the Club's corporate account. At present, the minimum contribution for Moy-Savings members is $20 per member per month. The average monthly contribution for investment clubs is $35 per month. Greater contributions in multiples of $20 are, however, welcomed and encouraged, but Moy-Savings set the minimum contribution at $20 (which is less than $1.00 a day per month) to accommodate members at different and minimum earning levels, as well as to accommodate temporary circumstances that might make greater contributions difficult or impossible.

Monthly contributions are mailed or delivered to the Club Treasurer on or before the 15th day of each month. For accounting purposes, there is a capital account maintained in the name of each member. Any increase or decrease in the corporate account is credited or debited to each member's capital account in proportion to the value of each member's capital account as of the valuation date. The valuation date is determined as of ten (10) business days preceding the date of each periodic membership meeting. Each member's contribution to, or withdrawal from, the corporate account is also credited or debited, respectively, to that member's capital account. Any other method of valuating a member's capital account, however, may be substituted for the foregoing method in accordance with the By-Laws of the Corporation.

The monthly meeting is the highlight of a traditional club's activity and its primary purpose is to analyze securities, to report on stock performances and to make investment decisions. But, the members of Moy-Savings reside in three (3) different states, which does not lend itself to monthly membership meetings. Therefore, unlike a traditional club, Moy-Savings elected five (5) of its members to serve on an Investment Committee which is charged with the management and investment of that portion of the corporate account designated by the general membership for investing.

The essential difference between the early investment club and the modern-day club is the emphasis on investment education. However, the most distinguishing factor between Moy-Savings and other investment clubs is the ability of Moy-Savings members to obtain emergency loans. Moy-Savings members are encouraged to borrow from the Corporation, at least on an emergency basis, rather than withdraw from their individual capital accounts. The loans are secured by the capital accounts, thus the Corporation assumes no risk in making the loans. More importantly, the borrower repays the loan with interest; consequently everyone, including the borrower and the Corporation, benefits from the loan as it is being repaid. The ability to borrow money contributed when needed has helped to bind the Moy-Savings members to the goals and objectives of the Corporation, and has encouraged consistent contributions into the corporate account. (The operation of the Loan Committee is discussed in more detail in Chapter 9).

Typically, everything in the corporate account is invested, except for a pre-determined amount reserved for emergency loans. The amount available for emergency loans is reviewed each year and may be increased by a majority vote of the general membership. It is a goal of Moy-Savings to accumulate enough capital in the loan reserve account to make it possible for its members to someday purchase homes and automobiles, acquire credit cards, and perhaps, to educate their children through the success of Moy-Savings. Moy-Savings members aspire to offer all of these goods and services through their own resources and then repay themselves with interest, instead of lining the pockets of unrelated or unaffiliated third parties with their hard-earned money.

Each member participates in the management and conduction of the affairs of the Corporation. There are presently 13 active members of Moy-Savings, and one vote per member. Husbands and wives are counted as one member, but may split their votes into one-half votes each if desired. Except as otherwise provided under the By-Laws, all decisions are made by a majority vote of the membership present at the time a vote is taken. Of course, a quorum must be present at Club meetings in order for the membership to conduct business.

Moy-Savings has found it to be more efficient and practical with members residing in different states to delegate the management and conduction of affairs of the Corporation to various committees. At present, Moy-Savings has four standing committees: (1) Investment Committee; (2) Loan Committee; (3) Membership Committee; and (4) Publications Committee.

The committees typically consists of five members. The committee members are initially nominated by the Board of Directors and elected by the general membership. Thus far, vacancies have been filled on a voluntary basis. Some members are elected to more than one Committee. The committees meet as often as necessary to carry out the mission set by the Board of Directors for each committee. The committees often hold meetings by telephone. Committee members serve for a term of five years and may be re-elected for additional terms.

There are ten members on the Board of Directors. Currently, the founding members of Moy-Savings make up the Board. In order to maintain continuity of purpose the term of office for the founding Board members has not yet been determined and no new board elections have been held. Eventually, however, all subsequent Board members will have to be elected by the membership as required by applicable state corporate law. More importantly, today most club decisions are made by the general membership of Moy-Savings at annual meetings, thus the role of the Board has diminished.

As previously mentioned, Moy-Savings has annual meetings as opposed to the monthly meetings conducted by traditional investment clubs. (See Form 2 for a sample annual meeting agenda). The date, time and place for the annual meetings are determined by the membership at the end of each annual meeting. The logistics for the annual meeting may be changed, however, as needed by the Club President or the Board of Directors. Historically, the annual meeting is held in Detroit, Michigan where the Club was founded, every other year.

Annual meetings are generally planned around a weekend of family fun and activities. After the traditional family reunion activities have ended, and it is time for the meeting to begin, one can hear briefcases opening all over the room. Our meetings typically last 1½–2 hours, and it is incumbent upon the President to keep the meetings moving and on track. Members are encouraged to bring their children to the meetings so that the children will understand what we are doing, why, and how the club business is being conducted. Currently, Moy-Savings is looking forward to accepting its first member from the next generation since it is still for the most part a family organization. Membership in the Moy family, however, is not required and does not guarantee membership in Moy-Savings.

There are approximately 65,000 African-American churches connected with the Congress of National Black Churches, representing 250,000 church employees and in excess of 19 million worshipers. There are nearly a hundred different African-American fraternities and sororities, and countless other civic and social organizations operating in the black community. On an annual basis these organizations spend billions of dollars, collectively, conducting and attending annual conferences and meetings. Many even have regional meetings on a quarterly basis leaving large sums of money in the host cities. These resources, in addition to the tremendous financial expertise that exist among skilled and professional black men and women, can quickly and easily transform the economic condition of black folks in America. If more African-Americans formed investment clubs like Moy-Savings, and reserved some portion of all of the time spent attending annual meetings and family reunions for financial and economic development agendas the economic transformation of the black community would be unprecedented and historically unsurpassed.

CHAPTER 4

HOW SAVINGS CLUBS CAN EVOLVE INTO FINANCIAL INSTITUTIONS

One of the goals of the Moy-Savings Club is to offer its members many of the products and services offered by financial institutions. Moy-Savings is also contemplating and discussing the pros and cons of becoming a full-service credit union when it is able to meet the minimum capital and membership requirements established for federally-insured credit unions. Why?

African-American financial institutions are very important members of the United States business sector, and they are absolutely essential to the health, growth and survival of the African-American community. According to the 1994 edition of The State of Black America Report published by the National Urban League, Inc., financial institutions are important not only as businesses which employ people and earn money for their owners and employees, but the importance of black-owned financial institutions is magnified by the tremendous need for capital investment and economic development in African-American communities.[1] It is irrefutable that African-

American families and communities have experienced unconscionable neglect by America's financial institutions. Financial institutions form depositories for savings and their investment decisions affect the amount and mix of capital formation among families and within communities. If African-Americans are to become involved substantively in determining their depth and amount of participation in the U.S. economy, then the creation and viability of black-owned financial institutions is critical.

In the 20-year period ending in 1993, individually and collectively, black-owned financial institutions, (banks, savings and loans, and insurance companies) lost ground with regard to the number of firms and the proportion of industry assets held. Of course, the 1973 through 1993 period (especially the latter half) was a significant challenge to all financial institutions, with record post-depression failures among commercial banks and S&L's. As a group, the black-owned financial institutions have survived, but not without casualties. It is likely that black-owned banks and S&L's have already absorbed most of the negative impact of the transition in the financial markets over the last 20 years, so that the survival of existing firms and the viability of new firms is not uncommonly at risk. However, success will clearly depend upon the appropriate set of strategies which must be undertaken to regain and exceed past performance. In an article written for The State of Black America Report, William D. Bradford, Ph.D. advises that black-owned financial institutions will need to specialize in financial transactions such as gathering as many relatively small deposits of households and other economic units and combining them to support capital development through loans for businesses, personal and housing capital investments.[2]

---

1 *The State of Black America*, 1994 edition, p.33.

2 Dollar for Deeds: Prospects and Prescriptions for African American Financial Institutions, by William D. Bradford, Ph.D., reported in the 1994 edition of *The State of Black America*, published by National Urban League.

Moy-Savings strives to become a full-service financial institution for the benefit of its members. Offering loans, at least on an emergency basis, to the members of Moy-Savings is the first step towards this goal.

CHAPTER

5

Why Don't More African-Americans Form Investment Clubs?

According to a survey by Roper Starch Worldwide for Ariel Mutual Funds, African-Americans are less likely to own most financial instruments except for bank savings accounts. African-Americans apparently prefer low-risk investments with some commitment to social responsibility, and shy away from investments that can offer greater gains. This is even more difficult to comprehend in that today's stock market lists numerous stocks offered by socially responsible companies with significant growth histories and/or potential. It's also possible to invest aggressively and earmark a portion of the profits to satisfy social responsibilities as is discussed in Claud Anderson, Ed.D's book *Black Labor/White Wealth*. Nonetheless, according to various surveys only 22% of blacks say they own mutual funds, as compared with 35% for nonblacks. In fact, African-Americans are generally under invested in the stock and mutual-fund markets, and more comfortable in CD'S, fixed-income securities and real estate. "These choices, however, keep African-Americans from translating recent income gains into long-term wealth, and from cashing in on the long running bull market," says Ariel President, John Rodgers, Jr.

Sadly, the idea of pooling funds for long-term investment purposes is also one of the primary causes for concern among African-Americans who desire to form an investment club. Another is as self-defeating as it is untrue, and that is the persistent belief among African-Americans that blacks are somehow culturally incapable of saving and investing money "together" as a group. Contrary to this common belief, Moy-Savings has learned from its research that similar types of savings and loan clubs are and have been very much a part of the African diaspora as well as virtually every other culture of people of color.

Long before the first investment club was established in Texas in 1898, people across the continent of Africa were ritualistically meeting to make contributions into what were commonly referred to as "pots." These "pots" were then bid upon by the various contributors, and distributed to one of them on a "winner take all" basis. The ritual was repeated every month until every contributing member received a "pot." There were no deposit slips, no written agreements, nor even a single inquiry as to how the money or "pot" would be spent. The contributors were bound only by their trust that everyone would continue to participate and contribute to the pot until everyone won a pot. This practice continues today across the African continent.

For example, such a practice exists in South Africa, where blacks earn and have very little money, if any, and until recently, were prohibited by law from owning land. In fact, black South Africans were otherwise prevented from participating in any meaningful way in the economy of the country. Yet, there exists among black South Africans an underground world of finance and economic development that thrived even while the apartheid government was in power. These ancient South

African investment clubs are called "Stokvels." The Stockvel "pots" are used today to start all types of businesses such as hawking, welding, carpentry, sewing, and a host of other informal and basic need driven industries, and were once used to support and protect the members of the African National Council. As is common in other parts of Africa, after every one who contributes has received a Stokvel pot the process begins again. Stokvel members are encouraged to make increasingly greater contributions into their Stokvels so that they can expand their businesses. And, of course, by creating larger Stokvels they can more quickly begin to progress upward both personally and communally in the economic and political evolvement of the country. Moreover, Stokvels also provide thousands of jobs for black South Africans. Indeed, it is the Stokvel system that has formed the basis for the most effective economic development programs for black South Africans today.

In other African countries and throughout the Caribbean, these savings and investment clubs may be called "su-sus." In other parts of the world where a large percentage of the people are economically challenged, these clubs are called "huis" as in China, or "kaes" in Korea, or "tanomoshi" in Japan, and "hoie" in Vietnam. Likewise, literally hundreds of thousands of small businesses in the U.S. have been financed and built by Ethiopian, West African, Caribbean Blacks, Central American, Chinese, Vietnamese, Cambodian, Korean and Japanese immigrants utilizing these types of savings organizations. For example, it has been estimated that as much as $100 million is at work at any given time in the Washington, D.C. area by virtue of Korean kaes alone.

Ironically, a few weeks before Moy-Savings was formed, the cover story in the October 1990 edition of Black Enterprise featured the Evans family. The caption read: "The Family That Saves Together," and described how a 12-member African-

American family parlayed their $700 a month collective savings into a $2.3 million portfolio in just five years. Copies of this story were distributed at Moy-Savings' organizational meeting and continue to be distributed to every new member. Another success story is the Washington Women's Investment Club ("WWIC") which was formed in 1987 by twenty-one black women in Washington, D.C. In 5-years the WWIC built a portfolio totaling $150,000, and they have consistently experienced an impressive 20% annual return on their investments.

In the final analysis, one must conclude that there are many more reasons for African-Americans to save and invest together than not; and it is in our collective interest to overcome our fears and distrust for one another in order to achieve common goals and improve our common good.

The NAIC has more than 12,000 club members, 50,000 individuals, and over 200 corporate members. Isn't it time for African-American savings and investment clubs to be more prominent among them?

CHAPTER

6

How to Research and Select Stocks

The first thing a club should do before making a single investment decision is to establish an investment strategy. Here are the four investment strategies considered by Moy-Savings:

1. *Conservative*—for investors who need current income and are reluctant to risk loss of capital.
2. *Moderately Conservative*—for investors who seek current income, but also place secondary emphasis on long-term capital growth.
3. *Moderately Aggressive*—for investors who seek long-term capital growth, with secondary emphasis on current income.
4. *Aggressive*—for investors who want to pursue maximum growth of capital, accepting occasional losses in exchange for greater rewards.

Moy-Savings decided to pursue an Aggressive investment strategy.

In carrying out an investment strategy, the following principles will produce the best results for most clubs: (1) invest regularly; (2) reinvest all earnings; (3) invest in "growth" companies; and (4) diversify, i.e. make different types of investments and invest in more than one industry. A club should establish an investment strategy and commit to follow the foregoing principles at the very first meeting. Setting short-term and long-term investment goals is one way of measuring whether or not your club is successfully carrying out its investment strategy. The NAIC suggests that clubs establish a target investment goal of 100% price appreciation for every five (5) years, which translates to a growth rate of 14.4% per year. A 15-member club paying in $20 a month should reach $20,000 in five years. In addition to the long-term "target" goal recommended by NAIC, a short-term goal is adopted by the members of Moy-Savings at each annual meeting.

In carrying out the club's investment strategy, the proper study and analysis of each investment the club makes is essential. For example, the members should agree that no stock will be purchased until it has been thoroughly studied. As previously discussed, the members of Moy-Savings reside in three different states. Therefore, in order to facilitate the research and analysis of stocks, Moy-Savings established an Investment Committee which consists of five members. Investment Committee members are elected by a majority vote of the Club membership. Investment Committee members serve for a term of two years and are charged with the responsibility of researching, analyzing and selecting stock (and other types of investment opportunities) in which to invest the Club's money. The Investment Committee elects a Committee Chairperson who is responsible for assigning stocks or industries for each member of the Committee to research and analyze (you would not want two or more members duplicating efforts by researching the same stocks), collecting the stock research and analysis reports from each member, receiving recommendations from each member, and distributing the stock reports and recommendations to all members of the Investment Committee.

There are many different ways to research and analyze stocks, and over the years, Moy-Savings has tried several of them. You may need to do the same before settling upon a method that works best for your club. We established a 10-step method similar to the one recommended by the Beardstown Ladies Club, but we adapted it somewhat to make it work better for us.[1] The NAIC also offers a stock research package to its members, which includes the following forms: Stock Check List, Stock Selection Guide and Report, Stock Comparison Guide, and Portfolio Management Guide. Each member of Moy-Savings' Investment Committee has been assigned an industry and is required to identify and study two stocks in that industry using the following ten steps we adopted. All of the information needed to conduct a stock research following our ten-step method can be found in Value Line's Investment Survey. You will find Value Line at most local libraries and some banks. You will also need a calculator to assist with at least two of the steps. The entire research project takes about 30 minutes for each stock, and should be completed within 30 days. The cooperation and commitment of each member to complete the project on time is very important.

Step 1. **Price**. Try to find two stocks in your industry that is trading around $25 or less. Check the Sunday edition of your local newspaper, The Wall Street Journal, Money Magazine, Standard & Poor's Report, or your personal stockbroker for suggestions.

Step 2. **Industry Ranking**. Record each company's industry ranking in Value Line's Survey. We look for stocks that

1 The Beardstown Ladies' Common Sense Investment Guide, p.23.

Value Line ranks in the top third of the industry, preferably among the top 25.

Step 3. **Timeliness.** Value Line also ranks stocks between 1 and 5 for "timeliness," which is a prediction of "relative price performance for the next 12 months." In other words, how fast the stock price will grow relative to other stocks. We look for stocks that have a Value Line timeliness rating of 1 (highest) or 2 (above-average). Record rating for each stock.

Step 4. **Safety.** All stocks carry risk, but it is possible to calculate their relative risk. Safety, as measured by Value Line, is the volatility of a stock's price around its own long-term trend. The narrower the band of fluctuation, the lower the rating and the safer the stock. The wider the band, the less safe, and/or more risky. We look for stocks that have a rating of 1 (highest), or 2 (above-average). Record the rating for both stocks.

Step 5. **Debt.** Value Line also records the debt and asset figures for each company. Record this information for the stocks you are studying. We look for companies whose total debt is equal to no more than a third of total assets. You may need to use your calculator for this one.

Step 6. **Beta.** A beta is a number that compares the volatility (movement) of a stock's price relative to that of the total market. A beta of 1 means that a stock price moves up and down at the same rate as the market as a whole. A beta of 2 means that when the market drops or rises 10%, the stock price is likely to move double that or 20%. Record Value Line's beta number for each stock you are studying. We would be happy with stocks that have a beta between .90 and 1.10 because they are not much more or less volatile than the whole market.

Step 7. **Sales and Earnings.** Find Value Line's earnings projections for each of your stocks. We look for companies with at least five years of solid growth in sales and earnings, and whose sales and earnings are expected to grow by double digits in the next few years. The sales of a small company should be projected to grow 12%; a medium-sized company should grow 10–12%; for a large established company 7–10% growth is good. You may need to do a little calculation for this step.

Step 8. **Price/Earnings Ratio**. The Price/Earnings Ratio is the price of the stock divided by earnings per share. The ratio determines the cost of a stock relative to its projected earnings. Record the P/E ratio for the last five years for each stock you are studying. Value Line lists average annual P/E ratios going back 15 years. We look for stocks that have a P/E ratio at or above the average for the five-year period. You can determine this by adding up the annual P/E ratios and then dividing the answer by five. We want to avoid stocks with a current P/E ratio that is higher than its average P/E ratio. After recording the average P/E ratio and the current P/E ratio for each stock, make a note as to whether the current P/E ratio is higher or lower than the average.

Step 9. **Upside-Down Ratio**. The Upside-down ratio tells us whether the stock's price is more likely to rise than fall. A *3 to 1* potential upside in the projected depreciation of the stock is preferred. You can find projected highs and lows listed in Value Line. Here's how to calculate this ratio: Let's assume the projected high price of one of your stocks is $40. Subtract the present price of say $15, which leaves $30. Now take the present price of $15 and subtract the projected low price of say $10, which leaves $5. Now, divide the $30 (upside potential) by the $5 (downside potential). This gives you a 6/1 ratio, and a very good buy.

Step 10. **Verify Price**. Even if one or both of your stocks have good growth potential and appears to be safe, the price may be too high, at least at the present time. In other words, you may have found the right stock, but now is the wrong *time* to buy it. So, you have to examine the price more closely. Record the high and low prices for each of the past five years as recorded in Value Line. If the current price is near the five-year high, you should think twice about recommending purchase of this stock at that time. Next, check Value Line's projections for each price appreciation, both high and low for the next three to five years. If the stock price is projected to rise 100% or close to that by the end of five years, this may be a good time to buy it.

Well, that's it!! After completing the research, the results should be sent to the club members or President with your recommendations. If the analysis is sent to the President it should then be copied and distributed to the other club members. The Chairperson of the Investment Committee of Moy-Savings then arranges a conference call among the Committee members to vote on the best and final selections. Although as many as ten stocks may be recommended, no more than two to three stocks are purchased by the Investment Committee in any given month. The following month, the Chairperson assigns new industries or stocks to be researched and analyzed, or Committee members are asked to analyze stocks recommended but not purchased during the prior month. The exercise is truly educational and enjoyable. It is the Investment Committee's job to invest the money contributed and accumulated by the Club. The Investment Committee is certainly more confident about its recommendations and decisions after going through this exercise. Here are the industry assignments used most often by the Moy-Savings Investment Committee: (a) banks and insurance companies; (b) utilities (including communications companies); (c) retail stores (including discount stores); (d) fast-food and beverage; (e) auto (including supporting businesses); and (f) healthcare (including medical, drugs, and service companies).

No matter how proficient you become at researching and analyzing stocks ironically, the more successful you are, the more likely you will need to secure the services of a good stockbroker. A qualified stockbroker can be an invaluable asset to an Investment Club. A stockbroker should act as your coach, recommend stocks, act as a custodian for your securities, collect dividends and keep them in your account until they are reinvested, disseminate stock and stockholder information to you, and perhaps most importantly, provide you with a monthly statement of your investments. We are increasingly using the information supplied by our stockbroker to make investment decisions, which has saved a lot of time. We've also found his information to be as thorough and reliable as researching the stocks ourselves. The Investment Committee is still responsible for interpreting the information and deciding which stocks to buy. We use a Merrill Lynch stockbroker in Dallas, Texas, Jerome Caulk, Assistant Vice President and Financial Consultant. Jerome shares our interest in seeing more African-American investment clubs established, and has been an invaluable resource person for us over the years. More importantly, Jerome has a great reputation for substantially increasing the portfolio values for his clients in record time. In 1996, Moy-Savings invited Mr. Caulk and another type of investment counselor to make presentations at our annual meeting. Both presentations were excellent and very informative, and having similar guest speakers at annual meetings is something we certainly plan to continue.

CHAPTER

7

START NOW: IT'S LATER THAN YOU THINK!

Unlike traditional investment clubs, Moy-Savings emphasizes savings as well as investments.

Now consider the following hypothetical, which demonstrates not only the importance of having a savings and investment plan, but also why it is important to start saving today.

> Most of us never seem to have as much money as we'd like. Sometimes it's difficult just to cover the necessities. We may not have much left over for investing. Besides, NEXT year we expect to have more money for one reason or another and THEN we'll be able to set aside MORE to make up for the years when we didn't invest anything. BUT, is it really possible to make up for lost time? Let's just see …
>
> La Quisha invests $75 every month. But DeSean has decided to wait until he can "afford" to invest. In ten years, DeSean plans to start investing more than two and a half times as much as La Quisha does now—or

$200 a month. What will their investments look like in 20 years? La Quisha will have invested a total of $18,000 ($75 each month x 12 months per year x 20 years). DeSean will have invested a total of $24,000, which is $6,000 more than La Quisha ($200 each month x 12 months per year x 10 years). Assuming DeSean and La Quisha each earn 8.5% per year and contributions are made on the fifteenth day of each month, who will be ahead after 20 years?

	La Quisha	**DeSean**
Monthly investment	$75	$200
Start Date	Now	in 10 years
Length of time	20 years	10 years
Total invested	$18,000	$24,000
Amount in 20 years (8.5%)	$47,358	$37,894

NEED WE SAY MORE????????

According to a special report published by Merrill Lynch, over the past 40 years, the national personal savings rate in America has plummeted.[1] In the 1950's, with a booming economy, the U.S. savings rate averaged 9.1% of the net national product. Since 1980, that rate has plunged to an average of only 4.2%—among the lowest in the industrialized world. This low savings rate weakens our nation's productivity and under-

1 The Fifth Annual Merrill Lynch Retirement Planning Survey; also, contact Merrill Lynch's Marketing Services Group and request the "Family Savings Kit."

mines our global competitiveness. The current savings crises affects every family in America. And, African-Americans know all too well that whatever adversely affects America at large, adversely affects African-Americans "moreso." It means that, despite higher average income, most Americans will discover all too late that they are less well-off than their parents.

Without sufficient savings, it will be difficult or, perhaps, impossible to afford the things most of us truly desire such as: a secure home for our families, a good education for our children, and a solid estate to leave our heirs. Tragically, the lack of savings will also rob us of a comfortable retirement. Today, approximately one in seven workers is saving nothing at all for retirement and many who do save already know that they are not saving enough.

For most Americans, personal savings—not a pension or social security—will be their primary source of retirement income. That's why it is so important to plan, save, and invest today to insure a comfortable tomorrow. For women, the saving crisis is even more pronounced, because most American women will spend their later years of life alone due to a longer life span. Today, the average age of widowhood is 56. The ever increasing number of late life divorces has also exasperated the savings crisis for women. Add to that job discrimination, age discrimination, and unequal pay discrimination and it's clear that women have more and greater reasons to be concerned about America's saving crisis than anyone else. Therefore, women need to ensure that they and their families are financially secure; however, only 25% of American working women between the ages 25 and 64 are saving for their family and children, and only 30% are saving for retirement. The obvious result, combined with a growing retiree population, increasing longevity, rising health care costs, and a shrinking work force (relative to the number of social security recipients), is that this lack of individual preparedness will place a heavy financial burden on younger generations. Already, there are adults caught in a financial trap between two generations—struggling to support their children and their parents as well. Currently, babyboomers are not saving enough for retirement—that's 76 million potential burdens for our children to bear. The average 50-year-old American has saved only $2,300. Yet for most people, 33% of income during retirement comes from personal savings.

The Tuesday, January 3, 1995 edition of *USA Today* featured the Sullivans, an African-American couple that started investing $30 a month in 1972. Saving became a habit for the Sullivans of Ft. Myers, Florida, and they were big believers of tax deferred compounding. The Sullivans' total savings—$247,080—was invested in nine funds of which $141,330 was invested in tax-deferred accounts, and $80,000 in savings bonds. Their goals: Mr. Sullivan (60) wanted to retire in two years at age 62. Mrs. Sullivan (58) wanted to retire in seven years. Then they planned to travel and take college courses in history and art. Mr. & Mrs. Sullivan put 5% of their salaries into government employee savings plans. They each put $2,000 into their IRA's and mutual funds, and $10,200—11% of their $93,000 income—into other mutual funds. Whenever they received a raise, they tried to increase their savings by that amount. The Sullivans ended up with a retirement cache of $327,000.

CHAPTER

8

How to Use Member Loans To Enhance Club Funds

Loans, loan agreements, collateral and installment payments are Euro-American concepts. Contrarily, African cultures, both historically and traditionally, do not believe in loans. The money contributed to Stokvels, for example, was given to the winning bidder with the understanding that eventually everyone would win and ultimately the whole community would benefit from it. In that the African-American culture, is perhaps, more American than it is African, Moy-Savings decided to adopt the best traditions of both cultures, by incorporating lending into its savings and investment plans. At present, loans are available to the members of Moy-Savings only on an emergency basis. The amount that each member can borrow is reviewed and reset each year at the annual meetings. This is perhaps the most unique and distinguishing feature of the Moy-Savings and Investment Club. How loans are approved and repaid is discussed in more detail in this Chapter.

After completing all the research as to how to form an investment club, the history and benefits of investment clubs, and perhaps most importantly, reasons for the successes and failures of investment clubs, I remember feeling very regretful that my family hadn't formed an investment club a long time ago. Counting my parents, we had a perfect "10" members in our family which is what the NAIC recommends as a good number of members to start with. I must have spent hours lamenting over how much money we could have accumulated over the years. Finally, I was reminded of the old adage "better late than never," and decided to stop worrying about what didn't happen, and start making plans for the future. And, not just my future, but the future of my whole family. Well, I was convinced that we couldn't afford to lose any more time, or money, or forego the opportunity to do something positive for ourselves. But, there certainly was no guarantee that I could convince my six sisters and two brothers and their spouses, to commit to contributing a sum certain into a common "pot," on a monthly basis for virtually the rest of their lives, which would be deposited into a bank account to which only one or two of us would have access, and then invested by other members of the family who had little or no investing experience. With a clear picture of my task at hand, I decided to anticipate the objections beforehand and incorporate workable solutions into the Partnership Agreement they would be asked to sign at the Organizational Meeting. (See Moy-Savings Partnership Agreement—Form 1).

Let's face it, for the most part African-Americans are forced to live with uncertainty about their financial futures. This is true even when we are gainfully employed and enjoying substantial incomes. It should not surprise you to know, therefore, that most Americans are ill-prepared for expensive emergencies, catastrophic illnesses, death or disability of the primary income producer, or even retirement. Consequently, the inaccessibility of the funds accumulated in an investment club account is clearly a problem. The nature and reality of African-

American life in America makes it necessary for African-American investment club members to be able to access the money they have contributed to the club whenever they really need it. On the other hand, frequent withdrawals from the Club account would obviously interfere with the Club's growth and success.

Fortunately, when Moy-Savings was started I was an attorney in the Legal Department of a major financial institution, and at least one other member had been employed by a bank for a number of years. The two of us knew all too well that banks made a tremendous amount of money lending money and charging their customers interest and fees on those loans. The obvious analogy made it easy to see that authorizing loans as opposed to suffering frequent withdrawals was the solution to this problem.

Even I didn't anticipate, however, how good this solution would prove to be to our Club experience. I later asked a bank officer where I worked to show me how much the payments would be on a loan for $500 amortized over one year at the market interest rate, which was at that time 6% per annum. The payments turned out to be minuscule, not more than $10, but comparatively the interest earned on the payments for one year was significant. I then asked the bank officer to calculate the interest earned if we added a minimum monthly contribution of $20 back in and earned a minimum interest rate on the $30 payment over the course of a year. When I saw the results of this request, I knew right then that the members of Moy-Savings would have to be encouraged to request emergency loans as needed, as opposed to making withdrawals from the Club's account. As consideration for the loan, payments also would have to include the minimum monthly contribution of $20. A provision encouraging emergency loans was written into our original Partnership Agreement and is included in our

Articles of Incorporation. Here's how Moy-Savings approves and requires repayment of emergency loans.

First, we elected five members to serve on a Loan Committee. Secondly, a member simply needs to contact the Chairman of the Loan Committee and request a loan and specify the amount. The Chairman notifies the Loan Committee members that a request has been made, and if the request is approved by a majority vote of the Committee members, the borrower is sent a Promissory Note and Pledge Agreement. (See Promissory Note and Pledge Agreement—Form 5). Third, when the Promissory Note and Pledge Agreement are signed and returned to the Chairman of the Loan Committee, the Chairman of the Committee contacts the Club Treasurer and instructs the Treasurer to prepare and send a check to the borrower as soon as possible. Keeping in mind that these are emergency loans, the process is intended to be simple, easy, and fast. No application is required, and a loan may be requested by telephone. If possible, the Promissory Note and Pledge Agreement is faxed to the borrower for signature. If necessary, the check is sent to the borrower by Federal Express.

Ironically, no one requested a loan from the Moy-Savings Loan Committee for almost three years, even though the Club increased the amount available for loans each year from a mere $200 up to $2,000 per member. In fact, for a number of reasons I was the first to actually request a loan. Partly because I really had a temporary financial emergency, and partly because I wanted to test our loan approval procedures. I also wanted to demonstrate to the club members that loans were truly available to them when needed. Most importantly, however, I wanted the membership to see for themselves how the Club could make money off of its loans.

Since Moy-Savings was formed, only three loans have ever been requested; two were repaid over the course of one year as required, and the third was repaid within 60 days. In the unlikely event of late or missed payments, the Loan Committee has developed friendly reminder letters to send to the borrower. So far, the Loan Committee has had only one occasion to send one of these letters. I think our experience with making loans has been a successful and positive one, because our members are always reminded that when we borrow money from the Club we are, in essence, borrowing from ourselves and paying ourselves back with interest. The ability to obtain a loan when needed has helped to bind our members to Moy-Savings, and helped to insure consistent and increased monthly contributions.

CHAPTER

9

How to Select and Accept New Members

How, when, and whether to accept new members have been the most difficult questions Moy-Savings has had to address. Concern and consternation about these issues weighed more heavily than investment decisions on our Club members. For two years the floor was open for nominations and discussions concerning new members, but no nominations were made and hardly anyone really wanted to discuss it. But, the fact was that at least 2 of our 10 members were no longer active in the Club, and had missed the last two annual meetings. And, there was little hope that they would become active again anytime soon. Monthly contributions from all but 3 members had also declined and become less consistent. I was also concerned that too much of the work and enthusiasm for continuing the Club had fallen on 2 or 3 faithful members. We needed new members to re-energize us, to increase the amount of money we had to invest, and to help us to reach our goals. Finally, in 1992 I managed to convince Moy-Savings to at least establish a Membership Committee which was charged with determining on what basis new members would be accepted into Moy-Savings, and to investigate how new members are accepted by other organizations, such as fraternities and sororities, and, finally, to receive and handle new-member nominations in time for the next annual meeting. Just when I thought we were finally ready to move forward, to my surprise and dismay, over the course of the year, the Membership Committee decided that new members should not be accepted. (Ironically, 2 of the 5 members on the Membership Committee were otherwise inactive in the Club, but the most adamant about not accepting new members). I knew then that concern for this issue was much greater than I expected, and a full and open discussion was imperative no matter how painful or emotional. Fortunately, I had approached several members about the issue before the meeting so I was probably as prepared as I could have been to respond persuasively to all of their arguments. It helped that I was able to bring my parents around to my way of thinking about accepting new members before the meeting. It wasn't easy because they were passionately against bringing in new members. Mostly they felt we needed to operate in a more business-like manner before involving anyone else. "We need to wait until we have ourselves together," my parents warned. But, I knew that they just as passionately wanted the Club to continue. My husband, Ed, and I showed them how contributions were continuing to decline. I described how all of the work was being done by 2 or 3 members who would soon tire of being overburdened. I made it clear that the future existence of the Club was at stake. Still their response was: "Everyone will just have to start helping out, but for now we need to keep it just among ourselves, just in the family." I pressed on by pointing out that everyone in the family was not as committed to the Club as some others. I was forced to hit them with the painful "reality" that some members (family members) may never participate in Club affairs again. Finally, I convinced them that accepting "new members" may be the only hope of bringing inactive family members back into the fold, but clearly without new members the Club's future was very uncertain. Other discussions primarily centered around concern for the family, or just wanting to keep things as they were, even though our quarterly reports clearly reflected that things were not as they were. Most surprisingly, the member spouses were more concerned about keeping it in the family than the others.

Well, despite my pre-meeting campaign, our 1993 annual meeting was our longest and most emotionally charged. In the end it all came down to an overriding concern for the family. No one wanted to offend the inactive family members, and almost everyone was concerned about involving non-family members. Fledgling though we were, there was comfort in the status quo.

While the Club may consist of family members, *it is not a family affair. An investment club is a business. It has to be operated and managed like a business.* You can be no less vigilant about handling the money received, or minding the investments made simply because the contributions come from family members. Moreover, you have to be realistic, there are some family members you can be in business with and some you cannot. Ultimately, when it comes to Club affairs you must stay focused on the goals and objectives of the Club, and learn to distinguish Club affairs from family affairs. By the end of the meeting, we had a unanimous decision to accept new members. Since the Membership Committee did not carry out the Club's original instructions, a more specific resolution was passed. This time the Membership Committee was charged to do the following: (1) develop a "new-member nomination and election form" which was to be distributed to the general membership on or before March 15, 1994; (2) instruct all members to send new member nominations to the Committee on or before June 15;

(3) copy and distribute all nominations to the general membership on or before June 30; (4) conduct an election of new members by a majority vote of the general membership on or before September 15; (5) report election results to the general membership and contact the new member nominees on or before September 30; (6) invite new members to attend the next scheduled annual meeting; (7) and instruct the new members to be prepared to make a lump sum contribution of $240 to the general membership on or before that date. We agreed that each new member would make a $240 lump sum contribution upon election, which is equivalent to our minimum monthly contribution of $20 for one year.

To assist the Membership Committee in its efforts, we established a Publication Committee, which was charged with developing and publishing a membership booklet to be distributed to each new member upon nomination. (See Form 7 for sample Membership Election form).

In 1994, seven new members were elected of which six accepted, and Moy-Savings had 16 members. We learned a lot from our first election so we refined the process for future elections. It was resolved at the 1994 Annual Meeting that new members could be nominated only every other year with the next election to be held in 1996; that until the next election the number of members would be capped at 16, except that new members may be elected during off-years to fill vacancies; and that new member nominations would be limited to one nomination per member; and, that the top 5 nominees with the highest number of votes would be invited to join the membership; and, that members may withdraw from the Corporation upon 30 days' notice of withdrawal prior to the end of each quarter, whereupon an inventory, review and accounting shall be done by the Finance and Accounting Committee and the withdrawal amount shall be paid on or before the end of the quarter. At the 1997 annual meeting the rules for electing new members were changed again after another lengthy discussion. This time new member nominations had been made and distributed, with elections to be held at the annual meeting, but the Membership Committee did not want to vote on the nominees for many of the same reasons that were raised in 1994. It was finally resolved, however, that the Club postpone and carryover the 1997 nominees to the next annual meeting; that the time for making nominations would be re-opened; that nominees must attend the annual meeting following their nomination, after which the members will vote on the nominations; and that the total number of Club members would be capped at 20.

Accepting new members in 1994 has turned out to be one of the best things that has happened to Moy-Savings. Our new members have helped us to realize and appreciate the uniqueness, value and importance of what we are doing. Of course, our contributions have more than doubled, and not just because more people are contributing. The founding members are also contributing more. Also, monthly contributions became more consistent once again.

We still have family members that are totally inactive in the Club. They do not make monthly contributions, attend annual meetings or participate on the committees to which they have been elected. How to deal with inactive members was an unresolved 1995 agenda item. It was my hope that members who miss 2 consecutive annual meetings *and* fail to make the minimum contribution of $240 for one year would be declared "inactive members" and ineligible to serve on Committees. But members who are otherwise active, but truly financially unable to make monthly contributions would be protected. Designating a member "inactive" would allow us to elect new members, who are interested, to serve on Committees of their choice, and allow the committees to function more effectively. The membership finally resolved to accept these ideas at the 1996 annual meeting.

We discussed another new idea at the 1995 annual meeting. It was suggested that we create a special membership for "heirs" as a way to further bind our Club members to the organization long-term. At that meeting Moy-Savings established new rules for "heir members." Heirs are allowed to apply for membership instead of having to wait for nomination, and may be elected by a simple majority vote, in addition to the top 5 new member nominees. We hope and believe that this concept of "heir members" will also encourage our children to participate in and continue the Club, in addition to strengthening the commitment of existing members.

At the 1997 annual meeting we established yet another incentive for members to stay active and committed to the organization. Since our children attend the meetings with us anyway, we decided that they should know more about what we were doing, how and why. We resolved to have a "Junior Member Program." All heirs between the ages of 6 years and 17 years of age are eligible to participate in the program. Participants are required to select a stock of their choice and to present to the Club members a brief report which includes the following information: 1) the call letters for the stock; 2) a brief description of the company and its products; 3) the stock exchange where the stock is traded; 4) the current, highest and lowest stock price; whether or not dividends have been paid and how much; 5) how the stock is rated. All heirs who make a report will receive a $25 US savings bond in his/her name. In other words the children will learn about stocks and receive savings bonds for their efforts. The Investment Committee fully expects to get good stock recommendations out of this experience as well.

When or whether you decide to take-in new members it's important to assimilate them into the organization immediately. The new members of Moy-Savings are assigned or elected to serve on committees as soon as they officially become new members. This is potentially a very divisive issue to wrestle with so be sure to approach it carefully, but don't be afraid to "go for it" if it will help the club to achieve its goals and objectives.

CHAPTER

10

You May Need a Publications Committee?

Moy-Savings is very fortunate to have a diversity of talents and experience among its members. The Publications Committee was initially established to develop a members' handbook to be given to each new member upon election. My parents, sisters and brothers accounted for nine of the original ten founding members of Moy-Savings. And the tenth member was just like another member of the family. The new members, on the other hand, could be friends or extended family members. Although we understood what, why and how we had operated for the past three years, it was necessary to provide that background information to prospective new members in a more formal manner. The Publications Committee developed a very attractive and informational Members' Handbook that both the new members and founding members have enjoyed and appreciated. The Members' Handbook contains a Welcome Letter to all prospective members which describes the purpose, policies, operation and benefits of membership in Moy-Savings. It also contains short chapters with the following titles:

(1) Why Was Moy-Savings Formed?; (2) Is Moy-Savings an Investment Club?; (3) Is Moy-Savings a Bank?; (4) Why Should Moy-Savings Become a Financial Institution?; (5) How Does Moy-Savings Operate?; and (6) Who Are The Members of Moy-Savings?

Our five-member Publications Committee consists of three educators, two Ph.D's, one attorney, and one award-winning songwriter and producer. This Publication was initially edited by the Publications Committee. The Committee also developed a logo and letterhead for Moy-Savings as our need to correspond with each other and others has increased.

CHAPTER

11

How to Leverage the Club's Long-Term Investment Goals

In addition to establishing short-term "annual" goals, you will want to set long-term goals. One of the long-term goals established by Moy-Savings is localization vs. globalization. Localization is simply investing in the economic health and stability of your own community. For far too long, African-American communities have fallen into disrepair and utter devastation due to economic neglect. But, haven't you noticed how every other ethnic group seems to get their start in America by heading straight for the nearest African-American community? There is money to be made in those communities. Just ask the Jews, Chinese, Koreans, and Arabs. It's as if someone told them at the Immigration Office, if you want to get started in America, open a business in an African-American community. They have money, they need everything, and most importantly perhaps, they'll buy anything!

One of the most memorable and moving speeches I have ever heard in support of localization was delivered by Floyd Flake, U.S. Congressman for the 6th Congressional District in

Jamaica Queens, New York, at the 1994 Congressional Black Caucus Prayer Breakfast. The speech was based on Ezekiel 37: 1–5, and entitled "Good News From The Graveyard." In the scripture God takes his prophet Ezekiel to a hill that overlooks a graveyard that is full of bones that have been there so long they have become dry. The Lord repeatedly asks Ezekiel whether the dry bones can live. Congressman Flake suggested that the same question resonates among American leaders, politicians, preachers, teachers, educators, social workers and psychologists because there are many of them who would classify African-American communities as "graveyards." To them there is nothing left in African-American communities but "dry dead bones." According to Congressman Flake, they have made that determination based upon statistics and data, which suggests to them that although there are people who are walking around in the communities, the communities are nothing more than graveyards. By way of example, Congressman Flake said that banks have made that determination, which is the reason they "redline" and won't invest there. And, corporations have made that determination, which is the reason that in spite of the fact that there is a major work force of individuals who, if hired, would make up a labor force that could make a positive difference in terms of our country's competitiveness, corporations will not locate there. He also said, "it is the reason insurance companies will not insure there, in spite of the fact that there are persons who, in many instances, earn incomes comparable to *other* people in other communities. They've already made a decision that these communities are nothing more than graveyards. But, these are the communities that you and I represent," he continues. "The communities the media writes about, and the newscasters talk about," protested Congressman Flake. "These are the communities where they believe the people are no longer human beings. They have declared that these are 'dry bones,' and that there is no need to respond to them because they don't really matter, and it won't make a difference. Can these dry bones live?"

Finally, Congressman Flake reminds us that before we can expect others to deal with this question, we must first deal with it ourselves. And, he continues, we cannot afford to believe that our communities are graveyards, because these are our communities, our people, our families, and our children. These are the bones and the remnants of those who represent us. "Do you believe that the bones can live?," Congressman Flake would ask again and again to which he finally answered, "everything that looks like a graveyard is not a graveyard, *and* anyway there's good news from the graveyard. But, in order to get good news from the graveyard you have to put good news into the graveyard." In the scripture, the Lord tells Ezekiel to speak and prophesy to the dry bones to try and bring them back to life. Ezekiel obeys God and the bones come together, but his words alone could not make them live. Likewise, Congressman Flake said, bringing life back to our communities is not just a matter of bringing the bones together. In other words, talking or preaching alone will not give dry bones life again. Just as family reunions and annual meetings of well-meaning civic organizations alone will not bring life back to African-American communities. And just as in the scripture the bones did not live again until the Lord blew new breath into them, which gave them a new spirit, likewise we have to blow new breath into the lives of the people who live in the communities others would call graveyards. And, for those who are the living dead in those so-called graveyards, we have to redeem them and bring them back to life. Thus, the good news from the graveyard is that we *can* breathe new life into the graveyard.

Well, localization is one way Moy-Savings has decided to breathe the new life into communities others might perceive as "graveyards." Moy-Savings resolved to identify the basic needs in various African-American communities, acquire and redevelop commercial property in those neighborhoods, and lease the property to selected vendors that will re-introduce the goods and services needed in that community. Localization vs. globalization. While everyone else is looking outside the United States to increase their wealth, Moy-Savings is focusing on the needs inside of the African-American communities, and establishing goals to meet those needs in new and innovative ways.

Once you have accumulated funds, you will be surprised how many programs and opportunities exist to help you leverage your money to do bigger and even greater things. Here are a few suggestions as to how to leverage your portfolio to achieve your long-term goals, create new opportunities in African-American communities, and increase your wealth.[1]

Dollar Cost Averaging. The Beardstown Ladies recommend dollar cost averaging for clubs or individuals following a conservative long-term investment strategy, and just starting to build a portfolio, because it establishes a regular pattern of investing, and adds to the power of your initial investment dollar. Dollar cost averaging is a stock purchasing technique wherein you make regular purchases of a particular stock or set of stocks with a set sum regardless of the market's level. Of course, when the stock prices dip, you will receive more shares for your money, when the stock prices rise, you will receive fewer shares. According to the Beardstown Ladies, over the course of an extended period of time during which stocks have moved up and down, the average price per share will be lower than the average for the trading period because more shares

1 Most of the information contained in this chapter is also covered in The National Telecommunications and Information Administration Office of Policy Analysis and Development, Minority Telecommunications Business Development Program, by Raymond Suarez, President, Quality Management International, and Robert Cull, Ph.D., Economist, OPAD, 1995.

were bought when prices were low, and fewer shares when prices were high.

Reinvesting Dividends. Instead of receiving dividend checks, another conservative long-term strategy, and one of the fastest and easiest ways of increasing your portfolio is by reinvesting your dividends. By reinvesting your dividends you will receive steady growth in your portfolio while compounding your income, because you will receive income from your initial investment and on the income from the dividend that the initial investment created. For example, the Mutual Investment Club of Detroit invested $291,045 over 52 years. The dividends gave them another $651,751 to invest, and a portfolio valued at $2,109,917, after withdrawals totaling $1,310,411. By arranging for automatic reinvestment of dividends you can increase your holding without being charged commissions on the new shares purchased.

Black Church Owned Nonprofit Foundations. It is estimated that the annual income of black-owned churches is $2–3 billion, much of which is invested in banks which are doing little to reinvest in our communities. So, more and more black churches are forming 501(c)(3) nonprofit foundations and community development corporations to engage in their own community development. In addition to private donations they are receiving sizeable federal, state and local grants. For example, the First A.M.E. Church in Los Angeles, CA. received a $1 million grant from the Walt Disney Company to create a microloan program which supplies low interest loans of $2000 to $20,000 to minority businesses. The program approved thirty-four loans totaling more than $500,000. The church's long-range goal is to capitalize the program with $10 million in private funding. If your church isn't ready to form its own community development corporation, perhaps there are 10 to 20 church members to start an investment club as a first step.

SBA Microloan Program. In 1992, the SBA launched a five-year Microloan Demonstration Program. Through this program the SBA funds loans to so-called micro enterprise intermediaries which, in turn, fund microborrowers. Microenterprise intermediaries are private-sector nonprofit organizations and community development corporations. Microenterprises or micro borrowers are businesses with fewer than five employees and initial credit needs of $10,000 or less. More than 96% of minority businesses in the U.S. fit this description. Perhaps, your investment club can become a micro enterprise intermediary and operate a successful micro enterprise program.

State-Funded Minority Business Development Programs. The City of Detroit discovered that over twenty percent of black business startups nationwide utilize at least some bank credit to launch their ventures, while less than ten percent of the Detroit startups managed to secure bank credit. In response, the Greater Detroit Minority Business and Industrial Development Corporation (Detroit BIDCO) was founded. Detroit BIDCO was organized under the State of Michigan BIDCO Act of 1986, which allocated $12 million to fund four minority BIDCO's. The four minority BIDCO operators can receive from $1.5 to $3 million in funding. State funding is made in a fixed rate loan for ten years, but with no principal payments before maturity. The loan can be converted into a grant if the BIDCO is particularly successful in meeting job creation and business development formulas. Your state also may have established a minority business and development corporation, and your investment club may be interested in becoming a BIDCO operator in your community.

Federally-Funded Community Development Programs. Before leaving Congress, Senator Don Riegle sponsored the Community Development and Regulatory Improvement Act of 1994. The purpose of the Act is to reduce administrative requirements for insured financial institutions to establish community development programs. The Act created a Community Development Financial Institution Fund to promote economic revitalization and community development investment through investment in and assistance to community development financial institutions. An application for assistance may be filed jointly by a community development financial institution and a community partner to carry out a community partnership. A community partner provides loans, equity investments, or development services, and may include a nonprofit organization. The target population includes individuals, or an identifiable group of individuals, including an Indian Tribe, who are low-income or otherwise lack adequate access to loans or equity investments. The Fund may provide up to $5 million of assistance during any 3-year period to any community development financial institution. You should determine whether one of the banks or S&Ls in your community is a community development financial institution or considering becoming one, and try having your investment club become the community partner.

Private Small Business Development Programs. GE Capital Services, a division of General Electric, operates a community small business development program that provides debt and equity capital, advisory services, and training assistance to small and medium sized businesses in urban areas. This voluntary corporate initiative seeks to invest $50,000 to $5 million per investment over 5–7 years in startups with verifiable contracts, or in existing companies wanting to expand, with emphasis on assisting minority and women-owned businesses. The company also profits from this venture. Your investment club could establish a similar program and experience comparable profits.

FINAL WORDS

In his 1967 speech, "Where Do We Go From Here?," Dr. Martin Luther King, Jr., issued this challenge to the black middle class: "It is time for the Negro middle class to rise up from its stool of indifference and to bring its full resources, its heart, its mind, and its checkbook to the aid of the less fortunate brother."

Forms

FORM 1

PARTNERSHIP AGREEMENT

OF THE

MOY-FAMILY SAVINGS AND INVESTMENT GROUP

This AGREEMENT OF PARTNERSHIP, made as of this 6th day of October, 1990, by and between the undersigned parties:

WITNESSETH:

1. Formation of Partnership: The undersigned hereby form a General Partnership, in, and in accordance with the laws of, the State of Michigan.

2. Name of Partnership: The name of the partnership shall be the MOY-FAMILY SAVINGS AND INVESTMENT GROUP.

3. Term: The partnership shall begin on October 6, 1990 and continue until December 31, 1991, and thereafter from year-to-year unless earlier terminated as hereinafter provided.

4. Purpose: The purpose of the partnership is to encourage thrift among its partners, create a source of credit at fair and reasonable rates of interest, provide an opportunity for its partners to use and control their own money in order to improve their economic and social condition, to invest the assets of the partnership, in stocks, bonds, other securities, real estate and personalty, to engage in any other activity, and provide any other service for the education and benefit of the partners.

5. Meetings: Periodic meetings shall be held as determined by the partnership.

6. Contributions: The partners shall make monthly contributions in such amounts as the partnership shall determine. Partners may discontinue and recontinue contributions as needed.

7. Valuation: The current value of the assets and property of the partnership, less the current value of the debts and liabilities of the partnership (hereinafter referred to as "value of the partnership") shall be determined as of ten (10) business days preceding the date of each period meeting. The aforementioned date of valuation shall hereinafter be referred to as "valuation date."

8. Capital Accounts: There shall be maintained in the name of each partner, a capital account. Any increase or decrease in the value of the partnership on any valuation date shall be credited or debited, respectively, to each partner's capital account in proportion to the value of each partner's capital account on said date. Any other method of valuating each partner's capital account may be substituted for this method, provided that, said substituted method results in exactly the same valuation as previously provided herein. Each partner's contribution to, or withdrawals from, the partnership shall be credited, or debited, respectively, to that partner's capital account.

9. Management: Each partner shall participate in the management and conduct of the affairs of the partnership. There shall be one (1) vote per partner. Husbands and wives shall be counted as one (1) partner, except that in the event of tie votes, Melvin B. Moy and Hazel V. Moy may vote separately. Except as otherwise provided herein, all decisions shall be made by a majority vote of the partners.

10. Sharing of Profits and Losses: Net profits and losses of the partnership shall inure to, and be borne by, the partners in proportion to the valuation adjusted credit balances in their capital accounts or in proportion to valuation unit balances.

11. Books of Account: Books of account of the transactions of partnership shall be kept by the partner in charge of Accounting, or his or her authorized delegate, and the Books shall at all times be available and open to inspection and examination by any partner.

12. Annual Accounting: Each calendar year, a full and complete account of the condition of the partnership shall be made to the partners.

13. Bank Account: The partnership shall select a bank for the purposes of opening a partnership bank account. Funds deposited in said partnership bank account shall be withdrawn by checks signed by either of two (2) partners designated by the partnership.

14. Broker Account: None of the partners of this partnership shall be a broker, however, the partnership shall elect an Investment Partner, and said partner may select a broker and enter into such agreements with the broker as required, for the purchase or sale of stocks, bonds, and securities. Stocks, bonds and securities owned by the partnership shall be registered in the name of the partnership unless another name shall be designated by the partnership.

Any corporation or Transfer Agent called upon to transfer any stocks, bonds or securities to or from the name of the partnership shall be entitled to rely upon instructions or assignment by the Investment Partner.

At the time of transfer, the corporation or Transfer Agent is entitled to assume (1) that the partnership is still in existence and (2) that this agreement is in full force and effect and has not been amended unless the corporation has received written notice to the contrary.

15. Compensation: Any partner performing professional services on behalf of the partnership shall be fairly and reasonably compensated and reimbursed for expenses.

16. Additional Partners: Additional partners may be admitted annually upon the majority consent of all partners.

17. Voluntary Termination: The partnership may be dissolved by agreement of a majority vote of the partners. Notice of said decision to dissolve the partnership shall be given to all partners. The partnership shall thereupon be terminated by the payment of all the debts and liabilities of the partnership and the distribution of the remaining assets either in cash or in kind to the partners or their personal representatives in proportion to their capital valuation accounts.

18. Withdrawal of a Partner: The partnership shall establish an Accumulation Period during which no withdrawals are permitted. After the Accumulation Period, any partner may withdraw a part or all of his interest. Partners are encouraged to request loans in lieu of withdrawals. Notice of withdrawals shall be given in writing to the Accounting Partner. The withdrawal valuation date shall be the first day of the month following the date of notice. Between receipt of notice and the valuation

date, the other partner's shall have and are given the option, to purchase the capital account of the withdrawing partner. If the other partner's do not exercise their option to purchase, then the partnership shall pay the withdrawing partner the value of his interest in the partnership in accordance with paragraph 20 of this agreement.

19. Death or Incapacity of a Partner: In the event of death or incapacity of a partner, receipt of such notice shall be treated as a notice of withdrawal. Liquidation and payment shall proceed in accordance with paragraph 18 and 20.

20. Purchase Price: Upon the death, incapacity or withdrawal of a partner, and the exercise of the option to purchase by the other partners, said other partners shall pay the withdrawing partner or his estate, as the case may be, a purchase price, when payment is made in cash, equal to ninety-seven percent (97%) of his capital account or his capital account less the actual cost of selling sufficient securities to obtain the cash to meet the withdrawal, whichever is the lesser amount. Said purchase price shall be paid within two (2) weeks after the valuation date used in determining the purchase price. In the case of a complete withdrawal in liquidation of a partner's entire interest, payment may be made in cash or securities at the option of the remaining partners. Where payment is made in securities, the full purchase price of the account will be paid the partner for that part of the account purchased with securities and the partnership broker shall be advised that the ownership of the securities has changed.

21. Loans: The partnership shall elect by majority vote a Loan Committee. The Loan Committee shall set the amount, terms, and rate of interest for loans from the partnership. Loans shall be secured by a proportionate share of partner's account or other collateral of equal value acceptable to the Loan Committee. Loans from the partnership are encouraged in lieu of withdrawals.

21. Forbidden Acts: No partner shall:

(a) Have the right or authority to bind or obligate the partnership to any extent whatsoever with regard to any matter outside the scope of the partnership business.

(b) Without the unanimous consent of all the other partners, assign, transfer, pledge, mortgage or sell all or part of his interest in the partnership to any other person, or enter into any agreement as the result of which any person or persons not a partner shall become interested with him in the partnership.

(c) Purchase an investment for the partnership where less than the full purchase price is paid for same.

(d) Use the partnership's name, credit or property for other than partnership purpose.

(e) Do any act detrimental to the interests of the partnership or which would make it impossible to carry on the business or affairs of the partnership.

This Agreement of Partnership is hereby declared and shall be binding upon the respective heirs, executors, administrators and personal representatives of the parties.

IN WITNESS WHEREOF, the parties have set their hands the year and day first above written.

PARTNERS: (Names)	ADDRESSES:
______________________	______________________
	______________________
______________________	______________________
	______________________
______________________	______________________
	______________________
______________________	______________________
	______________________
______________________	______________________
	______________________
______________________	______________________
	______________________
______________________	______________________
	______________________

MOY-FAMILY SAVINGS AND INVESTMENT GROUP

AGENDA

October 6, 1990

I. Introduction

II. Review Partnership Agreement

III. Show of Hands of Partners

IV. Adopt Partnership Agreement

V. Set Minimum Contribution

VI. Elect Partner-in-Charge; Investment Partner; Accounting Partner

VII. Elect Loan Committee

VIII. Elect Investment Committee

IX. Select Bank for Partnership Account and Authorized Signators

X. Sign Partnership Agreement and Receive First Minimum Contributions

FORM 2

MOY SAVINGS AND INVESTMENT GROUP, INC.

PROPOSED AGENDA

FOR 1994 ANNUAL MEETING

I. Call To Order

II. Welcome and Recognition of New Members

III. Approval of 1993 Minutes

IV. Financial Report

V. Committee Reports:
- a) Investment
- b) Loan
- c) Membership
- d) Publications

VI. Election of Officers

VII. Execution and Issuance of Membership Certificates

VIII. Goals for 1995
- a) new member goals
- b) new accumulation goals
- c) new loan reserve amount
- d) new investment projects or strategies

IX. New Business, Old Business, Closing Remarks

X. Adjourn

Please meet with committee members and prepare reports for the annual meeting!

FORM 3

MINUTES OF 1994 ANNUAL MEETING
of
MEMBERSHIP
of
MOY SAVINGS AND INVESTMENT GROUP, INC.

The annual Meeting of the Members of the Corporation immediately followed the annual meeting of the Board of Directors. The meeting was held on September 13, 1994 in Detroit, Michigan.

The following members, constituting a quorum, were present:

Melvin B. and Hazel V.	E. Barbara Wilson
Chris and Pam	Sylvia
John and Angel	Melvin P. and Barbara
Ed and Celeste	Merrill B. Sherman

The following persons were recognized and welcomed as new members:

Alexis Moy Kennedy, representing Kevin and Alexis Kennedy
Dianne Dove Houghton, representing Thomas and Dianne Houghton
Raymond and Judy Davis
Osia Vines, not present
Janice Meredith, not present

Upon motions duly made and seconded, the following Resolutions were adopted by the Membership:

RESOLVED, that the Minutes of the 1993 Annual Meeting held on November 25th in Vienna, Virginia be approved as presented.

RESOLVED, that the Financial Report through the 3rd Quarter of 1994 be approved as presented; and that Ed, Angel, Raymond, Melvin B. and Dianne were elected to serve as members of the new Finance and Accounting Committee; and that all members shall be assigned an account number and all new members shall be assigned an account number which corresponds with their nominator; and that account numbers shall be used in all future Financial Reports.

RESOLVED, that the Investment Committee Report be approved as presented; and that the Committee shall identify and recommend commercial investments for the Corporation for purposes of diversification, when the corporate income and earnings reach $25,000; and that Dianne and Raymond were elected as new members of the Committee.

RESOLVED, that the Loan Committee Report be accepted as presented; and that the new interest rate to be charged on all new loans is raised to 8%; and that a late charge of 1% shall be added to all loan payments made or received five business days past the due date; and that the following new forms shall be used by the Committee: Loan Application, Loan Approval Letter with Payment Instructions, Loan Payment Schedule, and Late Payment Reminder Letter.

RESOLVED, that the Membership Committee Report be accepted as presented; and that new members shall be nominated every other year with the next election of new members to be held in 1996; and that the number of members shall be capped at 16, except that, new members may be elected during off years to fill vacancies; and that new member nominations shall be limited to 1 nomination per member; and that the top 5 nominees with the highest number of votes shall be invited to join the membership; and that members may withdraw from the Corporation upon 30 days notice of withdrawal prior to the end each quarter, whereupon an inventory, review and accounting shall be done by the Finance and Accounting Committee and the withdrawal amount shall be paid on or before the end of the quarter; and that Alexis and Judy were elected as new members of the Committee.

RESOLVED, that the Publication Committee Report be accepted as presented; and that the Committee complete and publish the Moy Savings book for marketing and sale within 1 year.

RESOLVED, that the following persons were elected to served as officers of the Corporation: President—Celeste, First V. P.—Christopher, Second V.P.—John, Secretary—Barbara M., Treasure—Melvin B., Parliamentarian—E. Barbara W.

RESOLVED, that the Membership Certificates be executed by the elected officers and issued to the Membership.

RESOLVED, that the New Accumulation Goal for the Corporation shall be $50,000 by 1996.

RESOLVED, that the next annual meeting of the Corporation be held during labor day weekend of 1995 in Greensboro, North Carolina.

There being no further business to come before the Membership, upon motion duly made, seconded and unanimously carried, the meeting was adjourned.

____

Barabara J. Moy, Secretary

Approved:

____

Celeste M. Moy, President

FORM 4

(FORM 4.0)

ACCOUNTING REPORT *QUARTERLY CONTRIBUTIONS*					
			4th Qtr.	Total	Grand
Oct.	Nov.	Dec.	1996	1996	Total
60.00	60.00	60.00	180.00	660.00	3810.00
0.00	0.00	0.00	0.00	0.00	370.00
60.00	60.00	0.00	120.00	540.00	3820.00
0.00	0.00	0.00	0.00	60.00	1560.00
100.00	100.00	100.00	300.00	1040.00	2490.00
110.00	40.00	0.00	150.00	350.00	1230.00
40.00	40.00	40.00	120.00	320.00	1140.00
0.00	0.00	0.00	0.00	0.00	40.00
0.00	0.00	0.00	0.00	0.00	240.00
100.00	0.00	0.00	100.00	800.00	3690.00
40.00	40.00	40.00	120.00	440.00	1280.00
0.00	100.00	0.00	100.00	500.00	2300.00
50.00	100.00	50.00	200.00	820.00	1400.00
40.00	40.00	40.00	120.00	480.00	1320.00
0.00	0.00	0.00	0.00	0.00	560.00
600.00	580.00	330.00	1510.00	4500.00	25250.00

(FORM 4.1)

ACCOUNTING REPORT *INTEREST CALCULATION*					
Total	Cumulative	1st 96	2nd 96	3rd & 4th 96	Total 96
359.00	280.96	4.50	5.49	68.05	78.0373
81.50	69.52	0.71	0.82	10.46	11.9832
395.60	305.97	4.76	5.86	79.01	89.6260
184.95	147.87	2.18	2.53	32.37	37.0842
223.16	180.96	1.94	2.63	37.63	42.2022
117.71	95.22	1.32	1.53	19.64	22.4941
115.57	93.90	1.11	1.37	19.19	21.6702
11.21	10.06	0.07	0.08	1.01	1.1548
60.88	54.10	0.40	0.46	5.92	6.7836
356.58	280.43	4.30	5.21	66.64	76.1477
23.22	1.47	1.03	1.39	19.34	21.7539
47.91	2.47	2.17	2.99	40.27	45.4371
24.27	1.18	0.68	0.90	21.51	23.0865
23.99	1.44	1.03	1.39	20.14	22.5544
8.20	1.25	0.41	0.47	6.07	6.9486
0.00					
0.00					
2033.75	1526.80	26.62	33.11	447.23	506.9637

(FORM 4.2)

ACCOUNTING REPORT *LOAN PAYMENTS*				
Loan Payment January	Loan Payment Febrary	Loan Payment March	Total Loan 1st Qtr.	Grand Total 1994
0	0	0	0	0
0	0	0	0	0
0	0	0	0	0
0	26.50	26.50	53.00	53.00
0	0	0	0	0
0	0	0	0	0
0	0	0	0	0
0	0	0	0	0
0	106.00	0	106.00	106.00
0	45.00	45.00	90.00	315.00
0	177.50	71.50	249.00	474.00

FORM 5

ARTICLES OF INCORPORATION
OF
MOY-SAVINGS AND INVESTMENT GROUP, INC.

We hereby associate to form a nonstock corporation under the provisions of Chapter 10 of Title 13.1 of the Code of Virginia, and to that end set forth the following:

Article One
Name

The name of this Corporation shall be Moy-Savings and Investment Group, Inc. (hereinafter referred to as "the Corporation").

Article Two
Purposes and Powers

The purpose for which the Corporation is formed is to encourage thrift among its members, create a source of credit at fair and reasonable rates of interest, provide an opportunity for its members to use and control their own money in order to improve their economic and social condition, to invest the assets of the Corporation in stocks, bonds, other securities, real estate and personalty, to engage in any other activity, and provide any other service for the education and benefit of its members.

The Corporation shall do any and all lawful things that may be necessary, useful, suitable or proper for the furtherance or accomplishment of the purposes and powers of the Corporation, and shall exercise all powers possessed by Virginia corporations of similar character, including the power to own, lease, contract for the purchase and sale of, and to mortgage or otherwise encumber, real and personal property.

Article Three
Membership

Membership in the Corporation shall be through application to and election by the existing membership. Each member shall make minimum contributions into the Corporate account as may from time to time be set by the Board of Directors in accordance with the By-Laws. Each member shall be entitled to one vote in all matters coming before membership meetings, except that married members may split their vote such that each spouse has one-half (½) vote. Each member shall have full voting rights in accordance with the By-Laws.

There shall be maintained in the name of each member, a capital account. Any increase or decrease in the Corporate account shall be credited or debited to each member's capital account in proportion to the value of each member's capital account as the valuation date which shall be determined as of ten (10 business days preceding the date of each periodic membership meetings. Each members contribution to, or withdrawal from, the Corporation shall be credited, debited, respectively, to that member's capital account.

Any other method of valuating each member's capital account may be substituted for the method above described, in accordance with the By-Laws.

Article Four
Board of Directors

(1) The affairs of the Corporation shall be managed by the Board of Directors.

(a) The initial number of directors of the Corporation shall be ten (10). The number of directors may be increased or decreased from time to time by amendment to the By-Laws.

(b) The directors shall be elected by and at membership meetings.

(2) The names and addresses of the persons to serve as initial directors are as follows:

Name	Address
Celeste Moy and Edward Street	

Melvin B. and Hazel Moy

Pamela and Christopher Moy

Francetta Moy and Donovan Johnson

Barbara and Melvin P. Moy

Anita R. Moy

Sylvia R. Moy

E. Barbara Wilson

Merrill Moy Sherman

Angelica Moy and John Adams

Article Five
Registered Agent

The initial registered office of the Corporation is to be located at 1724 Abbey Oak Drive, Vienna, Virginia 22182. The name of the county in which the initial registered office is located is Fairfax, Virginia. The name of the initial registered agent is Celeste M. Moy, who is a resident of Virginia and a member of the Virginia State Bar, and whose personal residence is the same as the registered office of the Corporation.

Incorporator:

____

Celeste M. Moy

Dated the ______day of ______________, 1994.

FORM 6

Date: ___________
Amount: _________

PROMISSORY NOTE

For Value Received, the undersigned ("Borrower") unconditionally (and jointly and severally, if more than one promise(s) to pay to the order of ____________________, a ______________________________ corporation ("Lender"), at its offices located at ____________________, __________________, or at such other place as may be designated by Lender, the principal amount of __________________________ Dollars ($______________), or so much thereof as may be advanced from time to time in immediately available funds, together with interest on the outstanding principal balance hereunder, at a fixed annual percentage interest rate of _________ percent (______%), in accordance with the following payment schedule.

Principal shall be paid in twelve (12) equal monthly installments of $__________________ each, commencing on ____________________, 19____, together with accrued interest thereon and continuing on the same day of each successive month thereafter, with a final payment of all unpaid principal and interest thereon on ______________________, 19____.

Borrower agrees to make a minimum monthly contribution to the ___________________ of $ __________________ each, during the term of this Note, and hereby pledges _________________ of said Borrower's undivided interest in the ________________________ as collateral security for the due payment of this Note, and Lender is hereby authorized at anytime to set off and charge against said deposit account at or under Lender's control any and all obligations due hereunder.

Notwithstanding any other provision herein, Lender does not intend to charge and Borrower shall not be required to pay any amount of interest or other fees or charges that is in excess of the maximum permitted by law. Any payment in excess of such maximum shall be credited to Borrower's account or credited against the unpaid principal balance of the Note.

Borrower acknowledges having read and understood all terms and conditions of this Note, and hereby executes this Note under Seal.

________________________________(Seal)

FORM 7

MOY-FAMILY SAVINGS
PROPOSED NEW MEMBER INFORMATION SHEET
AND ELECTION FORM

NAME ____

STREET ADDRESS ____________________________________

CITY AND STATE ____________________________________

NOMINATOR ____

BACKGROUND INFO: __________________________________

____

____

____

YES_____ NO____

PROPOSED ELECTION SCHEDULE

1. New Member Information Forms Distributed by Membership Committee to Members by March 15th
2. Nominations Returned to Membership Committee by June 15th
3. Nominations Copied and Distributed to Members for consideration by June 30th
4. Responses Returned to Membership Committee by September 15th
5. Contact New Members, Give Notice of Next Annual Meeting, History and Operation of Organization.

FORM 8

Moy Savings and Investment Group, Inc.
Officer Nominations Recommended
by the Board of Directors

President:

____________________ ____________________

____________________ ____________________

First Vice President:

____________________ ____________________

____________________ ____________________

Second Vice President:

____________________ ____________________

____________________ ____________________

Secretary:

____________________ ____________________

____________________ ____________________

Treasurer:

____________________ ____________________

____________________ ____________________

Parliamentarian:

____________________ ____________________

____________________ ____________________

FORM 9

Moy Savings and Investment Group, Inc.
Officers' Ballot
Date ________________

President: ____

First Vice President: _________________________________

Second Vice President: ______________________________

Secretary: ____

Treasurer: ____

Parliamentarian: ___________________________________

FORM 10

CHECK AUTHORIZATION
MOY FAMILY SAVINGS GROUP

	Names	Check
Authorization requested by:	_______	_______
Check Request for: _______________	_______	_______
Amount of Authorization: $________	_______	_______

Approved by:

1. ______________________
2. ______________________

MEMO

Amount Issued: $______ Date________ ________ ________

For reconciliation, you must attach receipts, sales slips, etc., and return authorization form to Accounting within 15 days of receipt of check.

CHECK AUTHORIZATION
MOY FAMILY SAVINGS GROUP

	Names	Check
Authorization requested by:	_______	_______
Check Request for: _______________	_______	_______
Amount of Authorization: $________	_______	_______

Approved by:

1. ______________________
2. ______________________

MEMO

Amount Issued: $______ Date________ ________ ________

For reconciliation, you must attach receipts, sales slips, etc., and return authorization form to Accounting within 15 days of receipt of check.

FORM 11

MOY FAMILY SAVINGS
DEPOSIT/PAYMENT RECAP

Date:_________

NAME	SAVINGS DEPOSIT	LOAN PAYMENT	INT DUE	TOTAL REC'D
	_______	_______	____	_______
	_______	_______	____	_______
	_______	_______	____	_______
	_______	_______	____	_______
	_______	_______	____	_______
	_______	_______	____	_______
	_______	_______	____	_______
	_______	_______	____	_______
	_______	_______	____	_______
	_______	_______	____	_______
	_______	_______	____	_______
	_______	_______	____	_______
	_______	_______	____	_______
	_______	_______	____	_______
	_______	_______	____	_______
	_______	_______	____	_______
	_______	_______	____	_______
	_______	_______	____	_______
TOTAL	_______	_______	____	_______

FORM 12

MOY SAVINGS AND INVESTMENT GROUP

Loan Application

Date_______________

Name___________________________ S.S.____________________

Address____
Street City State Zip

Amount Requested_____________________

____
Signature

*Please note
Application can be made in person, by mail or telephone.

FORM 13

MOY SAVINGS AND INVESTMENT GROUP

Date_______________

Dear_____________________,

Congratulations!! As you requested, you have been approved for an emergency low-interest loan from Moy-Savings. The ability to obtain an emergency loan is one of the most exciting features of your membership in Moy-Savings. In addition, you will personally benefit from the interest earned on your loan.

According to the Promissory Note and Pledge Agreement you will be required to sign to receive your loan proceeds, your low monthly payments will include interest at the rate of ______% per annum.

Please remit your monthly payments of $___________ in person or by mail to:

Moy Savings and Investment Group, Inc.

C/O _____________________________

____

Detroit, Michigan _________________

on or before the ______ day of each month. A _____% late charge will be added to your monthly payments, if your payments are more than five days past due. We hope that you enjoy your money!!

Sincerely,

Loan Committee

FORM 14

MOY SAVINGS AND INVESTMENT GROUP

Date_______________

Dear____________________,

This is a friendly reminder that your ____(month)_____ emergency loan payment in the amount of $____________ has not been received and is now more than five days past due. Please pay the full amount that is past due plus a late charge in the amount of $__________, upon receipt of this letter.

If your payment has already been sent to us, please disregard this reminder. And, we thank you for your prompt attention regarding your loan account.

Sincerely,

Loan Committee

FORM 15

MOY SAVINGS AND INVESTMENT GROUP, INC.
LOAN PAYMENT RECORD

Date________________

Dear______________________,

Thank you for your payment of ______________,

	Amount Due	Amount Paid	Principle	Interest	New Balance
January					
February					
March					
April					
May					
June					
July					
August					
September					
October					
November					
December					

Any questions regarding this statement can be directed to any mender of the Loan Committee.

APPENDIX

Recommended Reading

Anderson, Claud, Ed.D. *Black Labor/White Wealth*. Edgewood, MD: Duncan & Duncan, Inc. 1994.

Beardstown Ladies Investment Club with Leslie Whitaker. *The Beardstown Ladies' Common-Sense Investment Guide*. New York: A Seth Godin Production. 1994.

Davidson, Joe. *"Shoplifting Black Dollars."* Emerge Magazine. March 1995.

Edelman, Ric. *The Truth About Money*. Washington, D.C.: Georgetown University Press. 1996.

Jennings, James. *The Politics of Black Empowerment*. Detroit: Wayne State University. 1992.

McLane, Helen. *NAIC's Investor Manual*. Naic 15th edition. 1992.

Naisbitt, John and Patricia Aburdene. *Megatrends 2000: Ten New Directions for the 1990s*. New York: Wm. Morrow and Co. 1990.

National Urban League. *The State of Black America*. 1994.

O'Hara, Thomas E., and Helen J. McLane. *Taking Control of Your Financial Future*. Burr Ridge, IL: Richard D. Irwin, Inc. 1995.